GAMES FOR
BORED ADULTS

GAMES FOR BORED ADULTS

CHALLENGES. COMPETITIONS. ACTIVITIES. DRINKING.

By Ian Gittins

EBURY
PRESS

7 9 10 8

Ebury Press, an imprint of Ebury Publishing
20 Vauxhall Bridge Road
London SW1V 2SA

Ebury Press is part of the Penguin Random House group of companies
whose addresses can be found at global.penguinrandomhouse.com

Copyright © Ebury Publishing

First published by Ebury Press in 2016

www.penguin.co.uk

A CIP catalogue record for this book is available from the British Library

ISBN 9781785033063

Printed and bound in Great Britain by Clays Ltd, St Ives PLC

Penguin Random House is committed to a
sustainable future for our business, our readers
and our planet. This book is made from Forest
Stewardship Council® certified paper.

CONTENTS

GAMES!

There are people who say that games are childish things that belong at children's parties. These people are wrong.

Games are far too important to be wasted on children.

Being an adult can be pretty boring. We all waste half of our lives doing 'grown-up' things such as commuting to work or filling in tax returns. We all need a bit of light relief – and that is where games come in.

Games are great fun. Playing them can keep you young (and yes, maybe slightly childish). Games can break the ice, keep you mentally alert, make the party go with a swing, and – this is the important bit – help to stave off boredom.

Games for Bored Adults is packed with games to help ease you through dull social situations and liven up enjoyable ones even more. It has top tips for getting parties started, surviving never-ending Christmases with extended family, or even having a laugh in – believe it or not – the office.

Even when you are already enjoying yourself, out on a stag or a hen night or simply down the pub, games can up the fun factor even further. So, why not ignore those dreary voices and defiantly play on?

You have nothing to lose but your boredom.

PARTY GAMES

Everyone knows that the best parties are all about getting drunk and trying to pull. Unfortunately, at the start of the party you will most likely be sober, and will need to find a way to get into the groove and lower those inhibitions. Which is where these games come in ...

PARANOIA

The players sit in a circle. Someone starts by whispering a question to the person sitting to their left, concerning the group playing the game. For example, 'who has the worst BO?', 'who has the hottest mum?', 'who spends the most time looking in the mirror?' The person being asked the question answers out loud. They then flip a coin. Heads, the questioner must reveal the question to the whole group, or tails they get to keep it a secret!

SIP SIP SHOT

This is a grown-up's boozy version of the children's classic 'Duck Duck Goose'. Everyone sits on the floor in a circle, while one player stands on the outside as the 'caller'. They walk around the circle patting the other players on the head one at a time, saying 'sip'. Each person the caller pats on the head takes a sip of their drink. At some point, instead of 'sip' the caller says 'shot'. That player has to chase the caller around a complete lap of the circle as the caller tries to get back and sit down in their place before they are caught. If the caller is caught they must take a shot. If not, the player they patted on the head has to take a shot and becomes the caller. You can also play this game with forfeits rather than shots.

YOU MUST
BE CRACKERS

This is one of those deceptively simple games that's a lot harder than it looks. Two players have 60 seconds to eat as many dry crackers as they can without drinking. A referee should be on hand to judge whether they have actually eaten their crackers or just sprayed crumbs everywhere. The winner can go on to play the winner from another match in a series of play offs, until everyone has a pounding headache.

THE PIZZA BOX GAME

You'll need an empty pizza box (just use the lid), a coin (larger ones work better) and a marker pen. The first person flips the coin in the air. Wherever it lands on the pizza box, draw roughly around it and write a challenge, rule or forfeit inside. Keep going until the box is full. When the coin lands on a spot the player that flipped it must do what the text says!

Some suggestions:

- the player on your right draws on your face

- everyone has to stand on a chair – last one up does a shot

- do a sexy dance

- wear your socks on your hands

- run outside and do a forward roll on the lawn

- kiss the player to your left

- sit under the table for the duration
of the next round

CEREAL KILLER

Players stand around an empty cereal box on the floor and take it in turns to pick it up using only their teeth. Only their feet can touch the ground, or else they are disqualified. After each round, cut two centimetres off the top of the box before trying again.

WARNING! This game carries serious risk of faceplanting the floor, and other funny but potentially painful hazards.

BALLOONATICS

Players divide into teams of two pairs – ideally, one male and one female – and each team blows up ten balloons. As soon as the game starts, they must burst as many balloons as they can between their chests, or any other part of their torsos, but they must not touch the balloons with their hands. The couple who burst all ten balloons first are the winners.

BEER PONG

Beer pong is usually played against an individual, or in teams of two. On each end of a long-ish table, place six or ten plastic cups in a triangle shape, pointing down to the opposite end of the table. Fill each cup about a third to half full of beer. You'll probably also want a separate cup of water to rinse the ball in – unless you're already so drunk you're past caring.

Decide who goes first, using the ancient code of scissors, paper, rock. The object of the game is to throw a ping-pong ball into one of your opponent's cups. When this happens they must drink the beer, and the player who successfully landed the ball gets another go. When the beer has been drunk from a cup, move it away and, if necessary, rearrange the remaining cups to keep them in some sort of formation. Or you'll be playing all night.

WISE
WANDS

This game requires the use of a roll of duct tape – and that everybody is drinking from cans. When players finish their drink, they must tape the empty can to the bottom of their next one in order to form their wizard's wand. The player with the longest wand is the wisest wizard and all of the other drinkers must obey his or her commands.

BLIND MAN'S SWAG

This game is played in pairs. One player in the pair puts on a blindfold (an unblindfold person from another team should check to make sure they definitely can't see). First, clear all breakable items from the room! Choose a 'swag' item that the 'blind men' have to search for. Bigger items are of course easier to find and smaller items harder. Blindfolded players should stand in front of their teammates, who, when the signal is given to go, must guide them to the swag using only verbal instructions.

THE MINE GAME

This is a great game for when you are about and about, and can go on for as long as you like.

The word 'mine' is banned (meaning 'that belongs to me' – not the hole in the ground, or an explosive device!). If anyone says 'mine' they must drop to the floor and do ten push ups, no matter where they are. Players can use a variety of cunning methods to trick fellow competitors into using the word. Sometimes a simple 'whose drink is this?' is enough …!

DRINKING GAMES

'In vino veritas', or, 'in wine, truth', the Ancient Romans believed. 'Alcohol! The cause of – and the solution to – all of life's problems!' added the great Homer (Simpson). Yes, we are never happier than when getting legless, so why not shed even more of your boring inhibitions and get stuck into some excellent drinking games?

SAVE THE QUEEN

Possibly one of the most annoying pub games to be involved in. If someone manages to throw a coin into your drink, they must shout 'save the Queen!', meaning you must instantly down your drink in order to 'rescue' the Queen from drowning. Key points of this game are that the coin must be thrown and not placed or dropped into the drink, and that any coins that miss can be kept by their target. So you might have to put up with a barrage of badly aimed change, but at least it's possible to make a small profit.

BATTLESHOTS

This is a fine drinking game based on the classic children's game Battleships. Two players both draw an 8x8 64-square grid and number it A–H down the left side and 1–8 along the bottom. The players then both write the names of ten drinks into individual squares:

- Pint of beer

- Pint of cider

- Jack Daniels and Coke

- Vodka and orange

- Gin and tonic

- Campari and lemonade

- Double brandy

- Glass of port

- Shot of absinthe

- Cup of tea

Concealing their grids from each other, the players take it in turns to name one of the opponent's squares: A3, B7, F8, etc. Every time they score a direct hit on a drinks square, the opponent must neck the drink. The winner is the first player to sink all of his or her rival's Battleshots. This can also be played in two teams, with players taking turns to call out squares and take the direct hits ...

EDWARD CIDERHANDS

When Johnny Depp was brooding through his lead role in *Edward Scissorhands*, he probably never imagined spawning this much-loved drinking game.

The idea is simplicity itself. Players duct tape a plastic 40-ounce bottle of cider (the game is sometimes called Edward Fortyhands) to each of their hands, and are not allowed to remove the tape until they have drunk the whole bottle.

How severely you want to interpret the rules is up to you. Some versions of the game allow players to remove the bottles to take phone calls or to use the toilet. Other, more hardline interpretations, say that doing so means instant disqualification.

The winner is the first person to drink both bottles of cider.

The wine-based version of this game is of course called Amy Winehands. Which would probably have given her a right old chuckle.

PUB
GOLF

This pub-crawl game requires a degree of pre-planning if you are to become a saloon bar Rory McIlroy.

The players need to map out a golf course of watering holes that they will visit during the course of an evening. They can play a 9-hole course, or go for the full, liver-obliterating glory of 18 holes.

In advance of your visit, each pub or bar must be given a par score of three, four or five. One or two of the watering holes should be designated as 'hole-in-one' special holes.

In every par-five bar that you visit, you are obliged to down your drink in five gulps. You can take four gulps at a four-par hole; three gulps at a three. Obviously, just as top golfers choose the right club for each hole, you should select a manageable drink for each pub.

In hole-in-one pubs, you have to down a shot in – you guessed it – one go.

Players keep a scorecard of their performance at each hole. They can attempt to down their drink in less than par, but any excess liquid down the chin results in a penalty stroke being added to their score.

To make it harder still, some holes are pre-identified as having a water hazard, which means that players are not allowed to use the toilet there. The winner has the lowest score at the end of the night, not to mention incipient alcohol poisoning.

GETTING FINGERED
(AKA MOST LIKELY)

Players sit around a pub table and take
it in turns to ask a 'Most Likely' question.
Some examples of this might be:

- Who would be most likely to rob a bank?

- Who would be most likely to go fox hunting?

- Who would be most likely to moon the Queen?

- Who would be most likely to spend
  a night in a police cell?

- Who would be most likely to find God?

The questioner then counts to three and everybody
points at the person they feel is most likely. The person
with the most fingers pointing at them has to drink.
The more fingers the more booze, i.e. if five people
point at him or her, s/he drinks five gulps.

FREEZE
FRAME

This game should unfold slowly over a long and bleary night. At the start of the evening, one person is chosen to be the Human Freezer. At a moment of his or her choosing, s/he must completely freeze. As soon as the other players notice, they must do the same. The last person to do so must down a shot and then becomes the new Human Freezer. Sadly, given the condition you will be in, you can expect to return home at the end of the night to a similarly frosty reception.

A GAME OF
TWO HALVES

There is no more enjoyable combination than drinking and football, and this game will heighten your enjoyment of any live TV match or episode of *Match of the Day*. Stockpile the ales, gather around your set with a few friends, and take a mighty glug any time a commentator or pundit says any of the following phrases:

- He'll be disappointed with that

- He's got no right to score from there

- It just sat up perfectly for him

- He's taken one for the team

- You don't like to see that

- I've seen them given

- He's got good feet for a big man

- They've been scoring for fun

- Game on!

NOTE: If the king of football clichés, Alan Shearer, is to figure in the broadcast, double the size of your drinks stash.

BUFFALO

Etiquette used to hold that a person always kept their right hand free at a social gathering so that they were able to shake hands with anybody they were introduced to. The old ways are sometimes the best, so any player caught holding their drink in their right hand for even a second must pay the instant forfeit of downing it in one.

In a more complicated version of this game players have to shift hands depending on the time. So, from on the hour to 30 minutes past, the drink should be held in the player's left hand. At exactly half past the hour switch to the right hand.

WHAT'S MY NAME?

At the start of the session, all players sit around a table and ask the middle name of the person on their immediate left. That becomes their own name for the night, and must be used at all times. Anybody who mistakenly addresses them by their real name shall pay a forfeit of a shot.

CALL MY BLUFF

Players take it in turns to tell the group three 'facts' about themselves. Two of them are true; one is an outright lie. For example, they might say:

- I was born with six toes on one foot

- I once stayed up for a whole week in Ibiza

- I didn't lose my virginity until I was 21

The other players then decide among themselves which is the false statement. If they guess right, the questioner must down a drink in one. If they are wrong, they must do the same thing. The winner is the last person to ten drinks.

BORDER PATROL

Players take it in turns to say the name of countries that they have visited. Any players who have never been there must take a hefty swig of drink. Players are disqualified from the game after their tenth swig, at which point they will be both drunk and deeply ashamed of being so poorly travelled. The winner will be the smug sod with the fullest passport.

('You've been to Burkina Faso? *Really*?')

VODKA ROULETTE

Depending on how many people you're playing with, you'll need a bottle of vodka and 20 shot glasses. Divide into two teams and fill up to ten of the glasses with vodka and the remaining with tap water. The players take it in turns to slug a shot and try to conceal from their opponents what they have just drunk (by keeping a straight face after vodka or miming a 'vodka face' after water. They can also double bluff). Players on the opposite team must identify the shot. One point for a correct guess, and the team with the most correct guesses once all the shots are done wins.

CENTURION

This is one of those challenges that sound pretty easy until you try it. The object is to drink 100 shots of beer in 100 minutes. On paper, this doesn't seem that hard:

- 100 minutes = 1 hour 40 minutes

- 100 shots of 25ml of beer = 2.5 litres, or 4.4 pints

But there's something about shooting beer that, after a while, becomes deeply unpleasant. You'll need someone to time the game, and enough beer to get through the game. No toilet breaks are allowed, unless of course you can take a shot with you and get back in time to do the next one. The thing that makes this game difficult is how fizzy beer is, particularly when drunk in a quick succession of very small gulps. Be prepared for the consequences, and stop if necessary. Many have tried, and failed. There is no shame in quitting Centurion to save your dignity.

OFFICE GAMES

All work and no play makes Jack a real drone, and as the office is sadly where adults are bored for the vast majority of their waking hours, five days per week, it would be foolish not to try to at least have a little fun when you're there. So, unleash your inner David Brent – but be warned that if some of these games go wrong, you may find yourself having far more spare time on your hands than you might like …

OFFICE CHAIR DERBIES

Sales pitches for wheely office chairs tend to emphasise dull qualities like their comfort and reliability rather than acceleration, torque or cornering ability, but don't let that stop you organising an Office Derby. Simply move a few desks, mark out a racetrack and install a hairpin bend by the printer. However, installing a pit lane by the water cooler for the intern to oil your castors may be taking it a bit too far.

LUNCH
LARCENY

Mess with the head of your office's healthy-eating nut
who brings in his or her own carb-free lunch every day
and deposits it in the exact same spot in the fridge.
Three or four players take it in turns to remove the
contents of their neat little Tupperware box and replace
the superfood salad with something else – a Big Mac,
say, or a Ginster's pasty. For added comic value,
leave helpful notes: 'The falafel was a little bland!' or
'Nice, but more salt tomorrow, please!' The winner is the
last person to be caught (and/or referred to
Human Resources).

CHEESY
PHONE CALLS

While a colleague is away from his or her desk,
change their answerphone message so that it asks
callers to 'leave me a message, beginning by naming
your favourite cheese'. The winner is the player who
manages to keep a straight face the longest when the
co-worker begins wondering aloud why all of his/her
messages begin with somebody saying 'Cheddar',
'Red Leicester' or 'Stinking Bishop'.

BULLSHIT BINGO

Meetings! If you have to endure these pointless gab-fests, why not actively enjoy them? Before trudging into the boardroom, arm attendees with a bingo card of the phrases and aphorisms that your boss is fond of spouting: 'Going forwards', 'Strategic staircase', 'Customer-facing', 'Brand actualisation', etc. The winner is the first person to tick off their whole card. You can't shout 'Bingo!' in work meetings so signal your win by saying 'I am looking at an optimised solution.' Good luck, going forward!

CARPET BURNS

A brilliant one for when all the real grown-ups are out of the office on a Friday. Players imagine that the office carpet is a seething pool of molten lava, and to touch it will mean instant death. All of your journeys to the kitchen, printer, photocopier or sales meeting must therefore be undertaken without touching the ground – whether you scoot around in your office chair, Dalek-style, or clamber over your colleagues' desks. You may choose to allow players to touch the floor in the toilets. Or, there again, you may not.

STRING
THEM ALONG

The players in this game have to imagine a piece of
string being tied at waist-height between two filing
cabinets in a main walkway of the office. To pass
through this space, they must either step over or bend/
limbo under this pretend rope – without being noticed by
any non-participants in the room. The winner is the first
competitor to pass through the space five times without
being challenged by a non-player. They then get to
keep the string.

AN
OFFICE GIG

Before heading into a meeting, award everybody a pop-star alter ego. They must use as many of that star's lyrics as they can in the meeting without being detected by the boss. If you are Bono, declare of an ongoing project 'I still haven't found what I'm looking for' or warn a colleague you will attend a conference 'with or without you'. If you are Beyoncé, brush off a minor setback by declaring 'I'm a survivor!' (You may find it harder to work 'I don't think you're ready for this jelly' into a marketing strategy session.) Anybody who sneaks in five lyrics without being rumbled by the end of the meeting is the winner.

NICK
NICK

This is a high-risk game for two players. Every time the managing director leaves his or her office, you must take it in turns to sneak in and purloin an item from their room. You have to then hide the item on your own desk (but it must be ON the desk, not in it). If you are caught, you lose (your job, most likely).

LOAD OF RUBBISH

Place a bin on the floor equidistant to, and within throwing distance of, each of the players. One player begins the game by copying all of the others into an email that says 'Load of Rubbish!' The other players must then immediately try to throw an object into the bin. The first one to succeed then has to send the next email.

PICTURE OF INNOCENCE

Get hold of a portrait photo of a work colleague – an easy task in these days of work intranets and Facebook – blow it up to A4 size, and print out 100 copies from the main office printer. When your co-worker is accused of gross egotism and misuse of company property, express innocent, baffled sympathy. You win, until s/he susses it was you and reports you to your line manager. At which point, you lose. Badly.

CROSSED
LINES

When you answer your phone, let your caller think that
they are overhearing the end of a shocking ongoing
conversation in the office before you greet them. You
might say, 'So, then I broke his arm with a claw hammer!'
or 'Ha! There is no way she can prove it's my baby!'
before seguing to a polite, 'Hello, can I help you?'
The winner is the player who gets away with the most
outrageous comment without being challenged
by their gobsmacked caller.

OFFICE
ROMANCE

Players take it in turns to bring a pack of Love Hearts sweets to work each day and, without being detected, leave one on the desks of all non-playing co-workers – from the managing director down. The winner is the last player to get accused of being the secret Office Cupid.

PAPER CLIP
DAISY CHAIN

This game is exactly what it says on the tin.
Raid the stationery cupboard and make a paper clip
daisy chain so big that it goes right across your desk
and onto the floor on both sides. Or wear it to meetings
like a metallic garland. Race colleagues to see who
has the quickest fingers, or just see how long
you can get away with it before your boss asks
you just what the hell it is you think you are doing.

FAMILY
GAMES

A lot of games in this book are based on drinking, excess and potential humiliation, and quite right, too. However, there is also a time for more – how shall we put it? – PG-rated games. And that time may well be Christmas. After all, you can only ask your gran about her sciatica so many times. So if you find yourself trapped with mind-numbingly tedious aunties, cousins and in-laws for days at a time, you might like to temporarily relieve the boredom by trying out a few of these games. They may even make Uncle Arthur and Cousin Ruth appear tolerable.

YOU'VE GOT
A LETTER

Players agree on a topic such as actors, pop stars, movies or football teams. One person names an example that begins with the letter A; the last letter of that word is the next player's starting point (so if the first player says 'Arsenal', the next person must choose a team that begins with L). Players have five seconds to think of an answer, or they are out. Out on their Arsenal, in fact.

ACTING OUT

Before this game, players all get together to draw up a list of 25 or so events that would trigger a strong reaction from anybody. Some examples could include:

- Being invited to Buckingham Palace

- Coming unexpectedly face-to-face with their favourite celebrity

- Getting caught up in a bank robbery

- Finding a dead mouse in a sandwich

- Winning the lottery

- Doing a bungee jump

The topics are put into a hat and players take it in turns to pull one out and act out how they would react – scream, cry, wince, foam at the mouth, etc.

The first of the other players to identify what they are reacting to scores a point.

HUMAN BUCKAROO

Wait for one member of your party to fall asleep: Grandad after the Christmas turkey will be a pretty safe bet. Gather a selection of assorted small items from around the house, which may include:

- Newspapers

- Ornaments

- Plastic cutlery

- Clean laundry

- Sunglasses

- Kids' toys

- Goldfish
  (actually, no. Not the goldfish)

Grade the items (one point, two or three) by their degree of difficulty and take turns to put them gently onto the sleeper without waking him or her up. If s/he grunts, twitches or farts as you do so but does not wake up, score a bonus point. The winner is the player with the most points when the (probably very angry) sleeper wakes up.

AFTER EIGHT CHALLENGE

Players tilt their heads backwards and put an unwrapped After Eight mint on their foreheads. The object is to be the first to slide the mint down your face and into your mouth without using your hands. Note that the faces you have to pull to achieve this are amazing, so it's a brilliant game for spectators too!

MIND
THE MAP

At over 150 years old and including 250 miles of track, the best thing about the London Underground is not the transport service it provides to the UK's capital city, but its odd station names and ample opportunity for puns.

Print out a large map of the London Underground and take it in turns to act out the names of different tube stations. Props are allowed: the only limitation is your imagination. Don wings and a paper halo for Angel; poke at the roses outside with your snooker cue for Kew Gardens; sit a toy clown atop a jar of pickle for (ahem) Piccalilli Circus. The other players shout out their guesses, scoring one point for each correct answer. Stations best avoided when playing with the family include Waterloo, Shepherd's Bush and Cockfosters …

DOCTOR, DOCTOR

One player is nominated to be the doctor and must leave the room. Everybody else must decide which never-before-seen, bizarre medical ailment they are all suffering from. Some examples might be:

- Believing you are Kim Kardashian

- Imagining that you have elephant-sized ears

- Fear of the colour red

- Believing the TV is a god, to be worshipped

- Having to SHOUT every third WORD that you SAY!

- An obsession with bananas

- Utter hatred of your left leg

When the doctor re-enters the room, s/he must observe the patients for two minutes then diagnose their mystery illness. A faulty diagnosis means they try again. A correct analysis means somebody else gets to be the doctor.

MYSTERY CELEB

Write the name of a famous person on a Post-it note and fix it to the forehead of one of the players, without them seeing what has been written down. S/he has to work out which celeb s/he has become by asking questions of the other players that can only be answered 'Yes' or 'No'. Players may wish to consider asking the following:

- Am I female?

- Am I alive?

- Am I a singer?

- Do I regularly appear on telly?

- Have I ever punched a TV producer?

- Do I have any super-injunctions out?

- Am I Harry Styles?

The 'celeb' has up to 20 questions to discover his or her identity. Note: It is best to give them people they will have heard of. It may be a stretch to expect Granny to get Lethal Bizzle.

THE
F WORD

One person is forbidden to say any word that begins with the letter 'F' (yes, including that one!) for five minutes. The other players bombard him or her with questions trying to make them slip up. They might include:

- What sport did David Beckham play?
  (a safe answer would be 'soccer')

- Which country is Paris the capital of?
  ('the one just over the Channel')

- What is the opposite of 'near'?
  ('distant')

- What kind of creature was Basil Brush?
  ('a puppet')

- What number comes after three?
  ('lots of them')

If the player on the spot is foo … er, tricked into saying a word that begins with 'F', or can't answer a question, they have F-ing well lost. Somebody else then takes over and the players choose another letter to be taboo.

SOCKOLATE

You need some pretty hi-tech equipment for this one: a dice, a plate, a knife and fork, a family bar of chocolate and a pair of clean socks.

Players sit in a circle with the plate, knife and fork, chocolate and socks in the middle. They take it in turns to roll the dice, with the object being to throw a six.

The first player to do so must scramble into the middle of the circle, put the socks on their hands and begin eating the chocolate bar with the knife and fork. Meanwhile, the other players carry on throwing the dice. As soon as somebody else throws a six, they replace the be-socked choc-muncher in the middle. The winner is … anybody who can emerge with the slightest smidgeon of dignity intact, frankly.

For an extra level of challenge add further items of knitwear – for example, a bobble hat, scarf, or even an oversized woolly jumper.

LETHAL LIZARD

One person who is going to sit this game out appoints one person to be the lethal lizard and one to be a detective. They tell everyone who the cop is – but the identity of the lizard remains a secret.

The players sit in a circle on the floor as the detective stands in the middle of them. It is his or her job to find out who the lethal lizard is and stop the spree of senseless killings.

Taking care to avoid detection by the cop, the lizard 'kills' its victims by sticking out its poison tongue at them. When a victim has been killed in this way, s/he must wait for a few seconds then groan and topple backwards out of the circle.

Can the cop halt this serial slaughter, or will the grisly gecko reign supreme?

LOOKING FOR BUBBLE

Each player is given a bowl containing an unwrapped
bubble gum hidden in a sea of whipped cream.
The first player to locate their gum wins. There is only
one minor complication: players are not allowed to use
their hands. Think of it as like bobbing for apples
– but far, far messier.

CELEBRITY SALAD

This game has lots of different names, but whatever you call it, it's a brilliant test of memory and mime skills for all the family. Start by giving every player six small pieces of paper. Without showing anyone else, write the name of a different famous person, or someone known to all the other players, on each slip of paper and fold it in half twice, putting it in a hat or bowl. Divide players into two teams.

Round One: Players from team one and team two take turns to pull names from the hat and describe the person. When they're teammates get it, they keep the slip of paper to one side. If they can't the player can pass and put the name back in the hat, but they can only pass three times in one go. Once the hat is empty count the slips that each team has. That's their score for round one.

Round Two: Refold all the slips of paper and put them back into the hat or bowl. Repeat the same process, but this time the player is only allowed to use one word to describe the person on the slip. Again, they can have up to three passes per go if their team can't get to the right answer.

Round Three: Put the paper back into the hat. This time players must mime the person written on the piece of paper they pull out.

Add up the scores from the three rounds to find the winning team!

BLOWFISH

Each player grabs a pair of scissors and carefully cuts a fish shape, approximately 10 centimetres long, out of one of its pages.

Line the fish up in the middle of the room all facing the same direction, like starting line of a race. Each player kneels on the floor behind their fish and, at a count of three, blows it towards the wall. The winner is the first paper piscine to touch the skirting board.

BALLOON TENNIS

Warning: this game potentially poses the biggest threat to Granny's ornaments since Geoff from up the road had a few too many margaritas and started demonstrating his golf swing in the front room. So it might be best to secure the area before play commences.

The number of people who can play depends on the size of the room. For a smaller room you may want to limit the number of players to two, and run a tournament.

Divide the room in half. (If it's Christmas, a piece of tinsel in the middle of the room works well for this.) The object of the game is to keep the balloon airborne at all times. It can touch the walls and ceiling but not the floor or any furniture. If the balloon touches down in your half of the room, your opponent gets a point, although no points can be scored from a serve. The first to ten is the winner, or alternatively, go the full Wimbledon and play a set!

STAG
PARTY
GAMES

The great British stag night traditionally involved fancy dress, ferocious alcohol consumption and stripper-grams, and ended with the hapless groom-to-be naked, covered in his own vomit and chained to a lamppost somewhere in Belgium. Well, no longer! Well-lubricated stag parties can now spend the evening engaged in a whole variety of dumb games that are just as immature and puerile!

MR PRESIDENT

The groom is the President of the USA, the best man is
his chief of security and the stags are his crack security
unit. If the best man raises his finger to his ear as if
listening to an earpiece, the stags must all shout,
'Get down, Mr President!' and leap on the groom
to save him from an assassin.

DARE CARDS

This requires a bit of preparation on the best man's part. Before the evening, he prepares a set of dare cards that a stag must perform or face a forfeit of a slug of Jägermeister. These tasks may include:

- Wear your pants outside your trousers (like Superman, you must change in a phone box)

- Stand on a chair and sing 'God Save the Queen' like the UK's strongest patriot

- Tell the barman you can only drink from a left-handed glass

- Greet a total stranger like a long-lost friend and insist on buying them a drink

- Compliment a stranger on his jeans

- Speak like a pirate for the next hour

- Sit under the table for the next 15 minutes

- Pole dance against an invisible pole in the middle of the bar

- Every time you use the urinal, drop your trousers and pants around your ankles like a five-year-old

- Dry-hump the fruit machine

- Borrow a bar towel from the bar and dust every table in the pub

Alternatively, these dare cards can be used as a forfeit in themselves for the losers of any other games, or just inflicted in response to any minor stag party misdemeanors.

JACK
THE LADS

You will need a pack of cards for this one. Shuffle the pack and deal the cards out, face up, to the stags. The only cards that are significant are the Jacks.

The person who is dealt the first Jack chooses a drink. The more potent it is, the better. Try suggesting a sambuca, or an absinthe (or, of course, a Jack Daniels).

The second person to be dealt a Jack must pay for this drink; the one who gets the third Jack must go the bar and fetch it (of course, this could feasibly all fall to the same person).

The person who draws the fourth and final Jack must down the drink. It's a dirty job, but someone's got to do it.

DIFFERENT STROKES

Before the stag night, the best man needs to get hold of a 'mankini' as modelled by Sacha Baron Cohen as Borat.

On the night, he chooses four of the stag party to play this game. They are all given a different swimming stroke: front crawl, breaststroke, backstroke and butterfly (do you know anybody at all who can actually DO the butterfly?). He also gives them all a pair of goggles.

At any point in the evening, if the best man yells 'Different Strokes!' the four participants must jump to their feet, don their goggles and mime their assigned swimming stroke.

The slowest stag to begin swimming is the loser, and must wear the Borat mankini until the next round.

GUY
GARVEY

How do you play a game named after the singer of Elbow? Easy – you ban a) pointing with fingers, and b) the use of the names of the stag party members. If you wish to address one of the stags, you must attract his attention by pointing at him with your elbows. If you forget, use those elbows to make a space at the bar as you pay the forfeit of buying a round.

TEXT MANIAC

The first rule of stag night is that nobody texts on stag night. Sure, there will be wives, girlfriends and lovers trying to get in touch, wondering where you are and itching to point out that you have now been missing for 72 hours.

However, any stag caught sneakily replying to a text shall surrender his phone to the rest of the group, at which point the game of Text Maniac begins.

The group can ask the victim to recite the mobile number of any of his contacts – old girlfriends, mum, boss, etc. If he is unable to do so, the rest of the stags can send them any text they want – and the phone owner is not allowed to read it.

WARNING! Be careful what you text to the victim's wife, unless you want him sleeping on your sofa for the next week or two.

I AM
THE FLY

Stags become flies for this game, which requires all of the stag party members to imagine themselves as buzzy, noisy pests (this should not be too much of a leap).

The best man should arm himself with a blue bottle (can you see what we did there?), which he taps to indicate that the fly game is about to begin. If he shouts 'Flypaper!' the stags must all leap to their feet and mime being flies trapped on a hanging strip.

This continues until the best man yells 'Rentokil!' at which point the stags must all fall to the floor, lie on their backs and kick their legs frantically in the air like dying flies.

The best man chooses the least convincing fly and tells him, 'You're winging it! You're having a larva!' At which point the loser buzzes off to the bar and gets a round in.

CRAP COCKTAILS

The stags put an empty beer glass in the middle of the table. Each tips a little of their drink into the glass (it helps if they are downing a wide range of different drinks – lager, cider, whisky, vodka, etc).

One stag then tips more of his drink – it can be a millimetre or it can be all of it – into the glass and tosses a coin. If it is tails, he must drink the entire glass in one. If it is heads, the next player to his right does the same thing.

The winner is the person who avoids drinking this deeply foul cocktail for the longest time. The losers … will shortly be feeling pretty horrible.

PANTY LOONS

The best man turns up for the stag night with a pair of women's pants. Where he gets them from is entirely his business.

When the best man says 'Panty Loons', each of the stags simultaneously tosses a coin. They compare the results. If there are more heads than tails, everybody who tossed heads is safe. The rest of the players go again, applying the same rules: if there are five stags and three toss tails and two heads, the tails-throwers are safe. The process is repeated until there is just one loser (if it comes down to two players, they must do a coin toss between themselves).

The losing stag must place the pants on his head like a hat and wear them until somebody takes pity and says 'Panty Loons', triggering another game.

How long you leave it before you do so is between you and your conscience.

YOUR CHARIOT AWAITS

You probably won't spend the whole stag night in one place, so why not liven up the otherwise tedious journeys between pubs?

The stags divide themselves into two teams, both of which must decide who is their lightest (or weakest) member. He then becomes the charioteer while the rest of the team is the human chariot.

The chariot must then transport the charioteer to the next bar: they can carry him any way they want as long as his feet do not touch the ground, meaning instant disqualification. It's a straight race between the two teams. The losers have to get a) their breath back, then b) the drinks in.

PEGGY MITCHELL

Named in homage to *EastEnders*' recently departed matriarch, this game requires one small clothes peg that shall be known as 'Peggy Mitchell'. One player must attach the peg to another's clothes without them noticing, then, after 10 seconds, point it out and say 'Peggy Mitchell!' That player then becomes Peggy and – much like *EastEnders* – the drama and intrigue rolls on.

SHARK ATTACK

The groom begins the night as the stag party's shark spotter. If he shouts 'Shark attack!' everybody must immediately get off the floor by jumping on to seats, tables, somebody's back, etc. while loudly humming the theme from *Jaws*. The last stag to make it to safety – as judged by the groom – becomes the next shark spotter.

TRADE
OFF

At the start of the day, or evening, the stag party divides up into groups of two or three. One member of each team selects an unseen item from a bag. The sorts of things that work well are novelty items, like a whoopee cushion or toy; food, like a chocolate selection pack. Be imaginative, but it should be things people (especially fellow drunk people) might want. Over the course of the stag party, teams should try to trade their items with people they encounter, the idea being to keep audaciously trading up with the aim of ending up with the best or weirdest thing by the end of the night, or a set deadline.

HEN PARTY GAMES

While the stag party is terrorising the local high street dressed in mankinis, the blushing bride and her entourage are demurely sipping white wine spritzers before an early night, right? Er, unlikely! In all honesty, the hen night is likely to be just as debauched as its stag counterpart, if not more so. Here are some excellent games to get the decadence going ...

PING-PONG TWERKING

Take an empty tissue box and fill it with ping-pong balls
– it depends on how big the tissue box is but 12 to 18 is
usually about right. Punch two small holes on one side
so you can pass a string through. Tie the string around
the waist of the first hen so the tissue box is behind her.
Start the music ('Work' by Rihanna being the obvious
choice) and time the hen as she attempts to twerk all
of the ping-pong balls out of her box. So to speak. Let
everyone have a go, and award a suitably risqué prize
to whoever does it in the shortest amount of time.

NEVER HAVE
I EVER

This is a classic hen party game. Armed with a shot, the hens take it in turns to say something they have never done, using the formulation 'Never have I ever …' Examples might be:

- Never have I ever had sex outside

- Never ever have I shagged on a first date

- Never have I ever been fired from a job

- Never have I ever been arrested

- Never have I ever got so drunk I wet myself

- Never have I ever faked an orgasm

- Never have I ever thrown up in a taxi

If any of the hens *have* done that thing before, they must 'fess up and drink the shot. If nobody is guilty, the hen who made the initial claim must drink hers.

SEXY CONSEQUENCES

This is a hen party take on the old parlour game. Each hen party member is given a strip of paper, and writes her name at the top before folding the paper over to hide it. Mix them around in the middle of the table so no one knows whose is whose. Each hen then choses a strip and writes a man's name before folding it again. She then passes it to her left and the process is repeated as everyone scribbles answers to the following questions:

- Where did they meet?

- What was the first chat-up line?

- What were they drinking?

- Where did they have sex?

- What positions were they in?

- What sex aids did they use?

- What did she say afterwards?

So the end result might be: 'Alice met Tom in a dive bar. She asked, "Is your packet as big as it looks?" They drank WKD Blue then went behind a bin and did the downward dog, with handcuffs. Afterwards, she told him: 'You've very nimble for a man in his seventies.'

Obviously, the game is more fun if it can be manipulated to feature men with whom the bride-to-be is known to have enjoyed previous liaisons …

MR & MRS

Before the big night, the maid of honour needs to corner the groom and ask him a few leading questions about the bride. She should film his answers on her mobile phone. Some good questions might be:

- Did they kiss on their first date?

- What is his pet name for her?

- What's her worst habit?

- What most annoys her about him?

- What is her favourite film?

- What do they argue about the most?

- If she were a celebrity, who would she be?

- What sort of drunk is she?

- What is she most scared of?

- What is her favourite sexual position?

On the hen night, ask the bride-to-be the same questions and then play her partner's answers. Every time that she gets an answer 'wrong', she drinks a shot. Every time she gets one right, the rest of the party do the same.

BAGS OF PROMISE

It is important there is no prior warning of this game before the evening. The hen-party organiser must confiscate each member's handbag on arrival and secretly remove the most embarrassing item from each bag. Later in the evening, these items are laid out on a table and the women have to guess what belongs to whom. Now, whose is:

- That KY Jelly?

- That picture of Justin Bieber?

- That bumper pack of 24 condoms?

- That half-eaten apple?

And WHO is so boring that their most outrageous item is an Oyster card?

ORAL
EXAMINATION

It is the maid of honour's duty to take a large courgette
and a pack of king-size condoms along to the hen night
and, at an appropriate point of the evening, produce
them with a flourish. Every hen tries to put a condom on
the courgette *using only her mouth*. Arrange a prize
for the quickest and a drinking forfeit for the slowest.
Note: any member who is unused to handling something
quite so big may replace the courgette with a chipolata.

YOU MAY KISS
THE GROOM

Should you have invited any maiden aunts along on your hen night, this is a tamer game (and what the hell were you thinking of, inviting maiden aunts on your hen night?). One of the hens must arrive armed with a huge blown-up photo of the groom's face. The hens all load up on lipstick, don blindfolds and do their best to place a smacker on the groom's lips.

LOONY
BALLOONY

The party splits into two teams, both of which have an inflated long balloon. The teams form two lines and must clench the balloons firmly between their thighs and pass them from one of the line to the other. If a hand is used, or a balloon touches the floor, they must begin again.

GOOD VIBRATIONS

This is the X-rated version of Loony Balloony. One of the hens brings along a vibrator (it may be better if it is unused!). Turn it on, and pass it around the party under your chins: no other part of the body is allowed to touch it. Impose a forfeit for anyone who drops it. When it comes to breaking the ice, satisfaction is guaranteed. Which, after all, is the point of a vibrator.

BOBBY VAJAZZLER

Thanks to *TOWIE*'s Amy Childs everybody knows all about vajazzling, but they can go other places as well as your lady garden! Take a bag of vajazzle gems to the hen night and give everyone five minutes to decorate their face or cleavage as amusingly as possible. The winner is the hen who gets the most laughs.

SEXUAL EALING

Give every hen a piece of paper and five minutes to compose a rhyme about a funny sexual experience. Like so:

> *I knew we'd never meet again*
> *I had this certain feeling*
> *I would never see Dave again*
> *Once we'd shagged in sexual Ealing*

Everyone then folds up their rhyme and places it in a hat. The bride should draw them out one at a time and read each one aloud to the group. She must then guess which hen penned which poem, with a forfeit for those she gets wrong.

TALKING
TABOO

Agree a list of words that cannot be said for the duration of the hen night. They should all be wedding-related: ring, service, dress, bouquet, reception, honeymoon, etc. If you want to be *really* hardcore, ban the word 'wedding'. Hens that forget and blurt out a taboo word must drink a shot. As the night wears on, this will be happening a lot.

PRIVATE DANCER

This is the bride's last night of freedom so let her have one last harmless fling. The other hens must choose the fittest, hunkiest man in the room and persuade him to come over and do a sexy (or funny) little dance in front of the bride. If they succeed, the bride downs a shot. If they fail, they neck it (the bloke might need a little Dutch courage, as well).

WEDDING DROSS

The maid of honour brings along a handful of
unlikely items that could be used to make a dress:
toilet rolls, tin foil, feathers, sequins, Sellotape, etc.
The hens split into two teams and use the bride and
the maid of honour as the models on which to
croate an alternative wedding dress.

SOMETHING BORROWED

At the beginning of the party, divide the hens into small teams of about three. Give each team a scavenger-hunt list of things they have to find in the course of the day. The only rules being that they are not allowed to exchange money for any of the items, and they can't be things that they already had on them at the start of the game.

The game works best if there is a mix of difficult and easy things, funny and strange, and items where the hens have to use their imagination! Some ideas:

- something beginning with Y

- something the barman has given you

- something orange

- something you can wear

- a business card

- a selfie of the team in the gents' loos

The winning team are the ones that either collect everything on their list or have the most items at a prearranged finish time.

WHO HAS?

All the hens write down a story of a memory they have with the bride. It could be good, bad or ugly! The pieces of paper all get put in a hat and the bride draws them out one by one, and tries to match the story with the person who she shared it with. This is a really good game for groups of old friends, and it could be worth warning party guests in advance so they have time to think of something.

ABOUT THE AUTHOR

Ian Gittins is an inveterate player of silly games, and a man whose research into the machinations of stag nights is so meticulous that he has been married three times.

Also by Ian:

The Periodic Table of Heavy Rock (Ebury Press, 2015)